THE

White Collar Club

Handbook

Ingrid Lederhaas-Okun

Printed in the United States of America

First Printing, 2017

ISBN 978-1-48359-320-3 (Physical)
ISBN 978-1-48359-321-0 (Digital)

BookBaby Publishing
7905 N. Crescent Blvd.
Pennsauken, NJ 08110

The Scarlet F

Welcome to the White Collar Club!

Unlike the Membership Only exclusive club you previously paid exorbitant annual fees to maintain to drink G & Ts with fellow MD's, VC's and manicured MILFs and DILFS, this club is paid for by Uncle Sam.

You are officially a felon, The Scarlet F, which entitles you to lifetime membership.

This Handbook is intended to help you prepare for your journey to Club Fed for those of you that are WCCs (White Collar Criminals) and, for Friends of F, this is intended to help you understand the sabbatical your friend is taking.

Let's Call It Dormish Modern

"Bienvenue au Marriott" is what you might encounter upon arrival at your Club Fed dorm.

The minimalist decor of your open space room is akin to your Freshman year Ivy League college dorm where you parents had the privilege of paying a healthy five figure sum annually, except your new temporary space will actually be nicer and cleaner.

You will be supplied with white cotton sheets and thick wool military issue gray blankets. On the positive side you don't have to worry about cleaning or soiling them, like your 800 plus thread count Pratesi linens at home, so lather up those legs and feet with Lubriderm from Fed Mart before sleeping.

Your room will be inspected weekly for cleanliness and you will have a fresh set of linens provided to you, another two aspects of life at Club Fed that are most likely better than the state of your Freshman year dorm, unless Mom lived close by!

Speaking of cleanliness, you will be happy to hear that you have complete privacy in the bathrooms and showers. Like College, at the end of the hallway you have two large rooms and showers (individual showers with doors and hooks for your robe/clothes) and bathrooms (individual stalls). These are open 24/7 for your convenience.

In addition to these facilities there is ample primping space available. Some locations have hair rooms with blow dryers, curling irons, flat irons and hair sinks for the women (and some WCC Men).

You will also have abundant sunlight when in your dorm, as there are large windows in the rooms (remember, you are at Camp where it is civilized, bars are for zoos) to better assist you when applying your facial products or styling your hair.

Also, like the Marriott, you will have large ice machines and hot water dispensers in your dorm. It's not Starbucks but you can begin your day with iced coffee and end it with hot chocolate, should you so choose.

Disclaimer...no two Clubs are the same. There are slight nuances (e.g. Danbury FPC has a salad bar, Alderson FPC does not) based upon how the facility is run. Many of these are privately run Camps. Yes, the US Government has outsourced! Your (for Profit) Camp is paid by Uncle Sam based upon how many days you are there, how many courses you take while on sabbatical, etc. So if you wonder why someone in Management at your Camp recommends you take a Beading Class, it's because they get a fee for it, not because they want you to regress to Kindergarten art class.

If any of you have been watching OITNB in preparation for your journey, you are unnecessarily alarming yourself. What is portrayed in this fictional show is just that, fiction. You have total privacy when showering or using the facilities. There are no Caligula inspired evening orgies. The experience is more akin to a Nursing Home environment (think Scrabble, Card Games and Knitting) than Bieberesque escapades.

What you will need to get accustomed to is the vast amount of time you now have at your disposal. It's up to you how to use it, but you will most likely never have an opportunity like this again to be able to do whatever you want for yourself.

WCCs are used to juggling a myriad of responsibilities and working (and playing) hard. There are no early morning or late evening conference calls to speak with your International counterparts, there are no fund raising events to attend in the evening nor any weekend sports tournaments that require your attention.

How you choose to spend your time is completely up to you, because as a WCC you will not be participating in the GED courses nor the Resume Writing classes offered to assist other Campers on re-entering the world post Camp (been there, done that).

The philanthropic side of you will want to assist with tutoring those less fortunate which can be very rewarding, but this still leaves you with a tremendous amount of time to spend on yourself. You can take this time to grow spiritually (hello Deepak Chopra), expand mentally (900 page biography...bring it on!) and tighten physically (Boot Camp has a whole new meaning at Club Fed).

Take it from WCC Hall of Famer Martha Stewart:

"When I was incarcerated at Alderson in West Virginia for a five month term, they had a ceramics class and in the ceramics class was a storage warehouse room where I found all of the molds for an entire large nativity scene...and I molded the entire nativity scene."

Not Your Father's Khakis

Khaki pants are a wardrobe staple for WCCs, whether associated with casual office attire or summers on the Cape. From a young age WCCs are exposed to khaki, beginning when their Mother dressed them in their first uniform for school to when their Father returned from a long day on the golf course in his best Greg Norman.

At Club Fed, khaki pants are worn for "formal" functions (Dining, Working, Classes). Upon arrival you will be outfitted with several sets of very durable pants and, in an effort to take the stress out of dressing, matching khaki shirts. The clothing provided is a cotton/polyester blend, with an emphasis on poly.

Think Dickie's, as Vineyard Vines and Bill's Khakis have not made it to Club Fed (yet!).

If this sounds vaguely familiar to you, it's because it is almost identical to the outfits provided to US Military recruits. Remember, Club Fed is Government run so Uncle Sam uses the same manufacturers whether for the US Military or The White Collar Club.

To complete the "formal" look you will also receive a pair of black rubber soled dress shoes and multiple pairs of thick white tube socks (think 1970's Larry Bird versus present day Cristiano Ronaldo in terms of appearance).

Fear not, there are plenty of casual attire options. You will also receive 100% cotton t-shirts in shades ranging from mahogany brown (new) to creamy mocha (used).

Given that WCCs are housed in Camps of the most minimal security and supervision there is no orange to be found. This is saved for those on a longer leave of a more serious nature. This comes as a great relief to WCCs as they can continue to associate their favorite French leather brand with this color versus their Club Fed experience.

You will notice that I haven't spent much time on undergarments as what is there really to say? Your Hanro and La Perla will have to stay neatly folded in your walk-in closet. Forget cleavage, Ladies will strut a uniboob in a jog bra while Men will stay secure in their tighty whities.

While you will receive your essentials, courtesy of all of the hard working US taxpayers, you can supplement your wardrobe with purchases from Fed Mart (more on this later).

How you choose to style your new label and pattern free wardrobe is up to you. You might find that you would like to highlight your newly taut

waist or defined arms. There are a variety of ways to personalize your monotone look. Channel your inner personal stylist!

It's as Easy as 1,2,3

When entering your retreat you might be surprised to find that you can easily walk on/off the property. Unlike your gated community at home there is no 24hr guard, no need for a security pass to enter/exit, no locks, no video cameras.

Most camps are in rural areas in counties you have probably only driven through en route to another, more enticing, destination. If you are coming from a city environment you will immediately notice the quietness and fresh country air.

Initial impressions range form pleasant surprise (flashback to Choate) to mild shock at your new circumstance. The hours spent watching Crime Shows were for naught. You are not surrounded by hardened thugs but rather Mothers/ Fathers, Sisters/Brothers, Wives/Husbands both young and old.

Instinct kicks in, the sisterhood/brotherhood goes out of their way to comfort you and help you adjust. Camps are reserved for primarily first time non-violent offenders. You will be surprised to find that many of your fellow Campers are University educated like you.

One of the biggest adjustments, besides your new monotonous wardrobe, communal living arrangement and lack of organic food products, will be setting your new schedule. Accustomed to a fast paced life you will need to adjust to a much slower pace and determine how you would like to fill your hours.

You can choose how you want to spend this time away from loved one. Parlez vous Francais? Habla Espanol? There are courses (primarily self taught) that you can take at your own pace. There are ample opportunities to practice your new language with fellow WCCs. You will be surrounded by people speaking a plethora of languages. To name just a few...Hindu, Yiddish, Korean, Japanese, Mandarin, Spanish, Patois, Hebrew and German. Yes, Club Fed is a cultural melting pot.

Language not your thing? Prefer to work out your frustrations doing something physical? Ask to work with the Landscaping crew. Some male facilities have construction crews that do everything from paving roads to pouring cement and will travel to other facilities to perform these duties. They also receive more compensation.

Yes, at Camp you can get paid!! Not only is Uncle Sam paying for your lodging, food and medical care but the Federal Government will also pay you to work. Granted, the sums are meager, but can be paid to burn calories and build muscles then spend your hard earned cash at Fed Mart.

Back to setting your new schedule. While extremely relaxed in terms of security, you will still need to work around a few set times a day when there is a general "count" to insure that the same number of people that were there in the morning are still there in the evening. This is a very brief exercise where you basically wait to be counted. Given that it is at the same time every day, you can arrange your exercise, language, etc. classes around this tedious necessity. Flashback to Grade School trips to the Art Museum where the teachers made sure the same number of people that left in the morning returned in the afternoon and if you ended up one short or one over (oh yes, hard to believe) there is a "re-count." Sadly, Math skills are in short supply at Club Fed.

You will quickly get accustomed to this daily activity. Should you be late/absent it could result in a "shot." No, not the good kind for your forehead creases, but a disciplinary black mark which normally results in you doing some type of menial task like rearranging the outdoor picnic tables in a star shaped pattern for no apparent reason.

Should the "re-count" not reconcile the disparity in numbers there will be a short period of time where you are asked to remain put while there is a general scramble to figure out where the overage/shortage has occurred. Normally it is some type of clerical error, but in the case where someone has taken a stroll off the property or just decided they wanted to go home early you might be inconvenienced a bit longer until that person is located. This is rather rare as wandering too far afield could extend your stay or be placed in a less desirable facility.

As a WCC interested in abbreviating your staycay it is not recommended that you take a long distance run off Campus nor miss any "counts." As you did at Boarding School, adhere to the house rules and stay under the radar and it will be smooth sailing.

Club Dred

The thought of being confined to Club Fed with a group of strangers is rather daunting and can conjure up images of being sent off to Swiss Boarding School with a suitcase and airline tickets and nothing more than a brisk handshake from your Father and a reassuring kiss on the forehead from your Mum.

In preparation for your staycay try to read up on your location and treat it like an adventure. Try to ignore the scathing blog posts and focus on the positive aspects of your new refuge. Miring yourself in negative thoughts and "what if" scenarios is not a productive use of your time or energy.

If Martha Stewart, goddess of pristinely organized closets and Michelin starred meals, can make something positive out of her staycay, than so can anyone!

Currently working 80 hr weeks and sleeping with your smart phone a short grasp away from you? Well, you will have a social media detox during your sabbatical. At first your fingers will be twitching for a keyboard and thoughts of Snapchat and Instagram will be running through your head, but eventually thoughts of FOMO will subside and you will be able to sit in silence and read and truly absorb a book without the sounds of pings distracting you.

You may also be accustomed to seeing movies on their release date, or a private screening at a friend's home. While that will not be the case at Club Fed, you will be seeing movies as soon as they are released on DVD. You will now have read all of the critiques before you see the movie so you will be better prepared to make your decision on whether or not the acting is Oscar worthy.

Rather than referring to your adventure as Club Dred, try to use this time away from home and loved ones as a time to meditate and reflect. Many people will envy (yes, envy) the chance to escape their everyday pressures and truly reassess their life...their values...their goals....and plan out how to be a productive and engaged person once you re-enter society.

In this fast-paced existence we are all running from one meeting/event/appointment to another and never really taking the time to pause, re-energize and re-prioritize our lives. Yes, the annual Canyon Ranch detox is nice, but it's really about losing the 5 lbs you gained over the holidays before swimsuit season, not about gaining inner peace. This staycay is really a chance to unplug and re-evaluate all aspects of your life.

Try to stay focused on what you can do that is in your control versus what is out of your control.

Good people make mistakes, that doesn't mean that they aren't still good people.

Color Blind
WCC's come from a rather homogenous coterie of like minded and like colored kinsmen. Club Fed is the UN of Clubs. Housed under one roof is a melting pot of people from a variety of different religious and cultural backgrounds. At first WCC's will encounter a bit of culture shock at their surroundings but very quickly will become color blind to their new fellow sojourners.

Slang terms abound, but suffice it to say that people of ALL races (and combinations thereof) have found their way to Club Fed.

Take this time to learn about different religious and cultural traditions. Celebrate Chinese New Year with the clique from California, try eating what the Indian ladies have spiced up from the offerings in Fed Mart and

learn a word or two of Patois from the Haitians....you never know when it might come in handy!

Time to throw away any previous conceptions you have about people or races....you will find that you have more in common than you realize. Yes, you may have grown up in vastly different worlds but the basic beliefs and needs we all have....love, laughter...you share.

iFed

One of the biggest challenges in our Twitterverse will be the lack of electronic devices and ticker tape news 24/7 on your sabbatical.

As a diehard WCC accustomed to juggling an iPad, MacBook and iPhone (not to mention your professional devices) you will want to have your WSJ subscription converted to paper form and sent to your temporary address. Yes, you can receive subscriptions at Club Fed. You can remain in the loop on all things WCC so that when you depart you can pick up where you left off.

You will soon find that Mail Call is one of the highlights of your day. Friends of F can send paperback books, magazines and cards. Sadly, no home baked goods are allowed, so Grandma's recipe butter crescent cookies will need to wait until you are back home.

You will also have access to a government monitored email but no access to the internet. That being said, while you have to pay for email (minimal charge) you can get your electronic "fix" by spending hours in email (if you so desire). Skype is also available should you wish to see family and friends but keep in mind they will be seeing you as well. If khaki is not your best color it might be best to stick with electronic and snail mail correspondence.

In terms of snail mail there are some basic rules, like you can not receive hard cover books from an individual but can receive hard cover books directly from Amazon. I guess they worry that your crazy Uncle Harry will try to smuggle you a few of his happy pills in between the book cover.

You will also have access to a Library. This is where Club Fed is not like your undergrad experience. The books in the Library look like they were donated several decades ago....you will now find where all of those encyclopedias ended up! More recent additions are limited to James Patterson and Stephen King novels.

To maximize you experience it is recommended that you stock up on all of those NYT Bestsellers you never got time to read due to your work/travel schedule. You will have more down time than you have ever had and given your OCD tendencies it's best to fill it with biographies, historical reference books and an occasional Nobel Prize winning tome.

If you are in need of Legal advice, there is access to a small Legal Library, but it's probably best to ask around as you will find a plethora of Legal WCCs in your midst. Judges, Lawyers, Probation Officers, etc. will all be sharing the same dorm and their advice is free and probably more relevant to your situation than the outdated information contained in the resource room.

Entertainment? Beside the daily goings on....each dorm has a room full of flat screen TVs tuned into different channels that you can access via your MP3 player. Be prepared, TV shows are selected based on a general consensus. You may not find that everyone shares your love of PBS but that a version of Bravo's Housewives is on regularly.

For some odd reason many of the requests are for Crime shows (CSI, Locked Up, Dawg the Bounty Hunter). Not sure if people are looking to see relatives featured or are riveted with the (inevitable) outcomes.

Movies are also shown weekly, normally the ones most recently released on DVD. You can either watch in your dorm TV room with a nice bowl of microwave popcorn or can walk across campus to a theatre-like setting set up in the gym (another disclaimer, not all Clubs have a gymnasium/theatre but if your Park Avenue Law Firm was worth the six figures you paid you should have a theatre)

WCC....Call Home

There are a multitude of methods in which to stay "connected" to your family and friends while at Club Fed.

Should your loved ones care to make the journey to your rural retreat and see you in person, versus the limited time on Skype, they are welcome to come every week should you/they so desire. In many cases the journey is long, as Camps are intentionally located outside of tempting/stimulating metropolitan areas (more *Deliverance* than *Gosford Park*).

Visiting rooms differ based on your location, but it's normally an open room with tables, chairs, perhaps an area for children with toys, vending machines, bathrooms, etc. There are no barriers separating you and, weather and location permitting, there could also be an outside area with swings, picnic tables and chairs to enjoy the fresh air.

You can kiss, hug, hold hands and relax in one another's presence. As with any shared social experience you should not exhibit excessive amounts of PDA nor behave in a way that would be offensive to others. Should you cross the line (ala Miley Cyrus) your visits will be curtailed.

Prior to entering the social gathering space your visitor has purged themselves of everything that could potentially be harmful. Similar to your TSA experience no liquids, etc. are allowed but can be purchased once inside.

As no hard cash is allowed at Camp, like your Club chit system at home, your visitors need to bring money for the Vending Machines. As there may or may not be a change machine encourage them to bring rolls of quarters so that you can indulge in your favorite forbidden childhood Hostess treats.

Visits can last many hours, depending upon when guests arrive and when they choose to depart. Hours can vary but assume a healthy 4-5 hour experience.

Should you wish to capture the essence of a visit, many Camps provide photographers to record the moment. Given that you will be swathed in head to toe khaki you might want to suggest your fellow subject matters wear something that compliments what you are wearing or they hide your attire altogether in a group shot.

Yes, some people wish to have photos taken on sabbatical...it may seem hard to believe, but there are ample photo opportunities available, not just during visits. One of your fellow Campers will have taken on the responsibility of the resident Canon Sharpshooter (the only type of sharp-shooter around) and will have set weekly hours when they will take posed pictures of you and your new friends.

For these occasions people prepare as if Annie Leibovitz had set up shop. Women spend hours on their hair and make up and outfits which have been set aside for such events are brought out and pressed until the creases are razor sharp.

Backdrops are provided as well....depending upon the season you might have butterflies brightly painted on a large canvas or a nativity scene during the holidays. Not exactly like the Scavullo portraits of Mummy in her heyday but something to commemorate your staycay as well as the new friends you have made.

Besides visits, you can also make calls. You will be allocated a certain number of minutes per month and it's at your discretion how you would like to distribute that time but no single call can last longer than 15 minutes. That being said, be sure your friends and family don't spend the first 5 minutes venting to you about the horrible weather they encountered on their recent trip to Parrot Cay and focus the time on topics of interest to you, like what ranking Jordan Spieth has achieved.

As Uncle Sam is providing the phones (a vast number in your new lodging) he also retains records of your calls, so don't joke about joining ISIS when you depart or you may experience an interrogation scene out of *Meet The Parents* explaining your attempt at comedy.

Crimson Calls

Accustomed to waxing lyrical over the latest trends or celebrity gossip? Well, one needs to be more conservative in their speech when speaking on the telephone at Club Fed.

Phone time is limited and seems to evaporate at warp speed when it is counted.

Individual calls are limited to 15 minutes and individuals are allotted a monthly total of 300 minutes* So, one can either use up all of their allotment in a few days or they can spread it out over the month.

Judicious thought needs to be given to whom and when calls are made so that it can be spread over a longer period of time.

Some people put together elaborate monthly plans allocating minutes by friend/family member as well as calculating the number of days between calls.

Uncle Sam is more generous with minutes allocated over the holidays knowing that more time may be needed to spread cheer. On average, 100 extra minutes* are provided in the months of November and December so that one can discuss all of the Thanksgiving and Christmas/Hanukkah/Kwanzaa events they will not be partaking in as a result of their sabbatical.

Keep in mind that the recipient of a call from Club Fed will hear a tape recorded message that they are receiving a call from a member of Club Fed and that they should be prepared to accept the call. Should the recipient not be available when the call is placed you will not be able to leave a voice mail message.

This scripted message can sound a bit ominous so it is best that the person receiving the call not put you on speakerphone or be in a public place when receiving a call from their Scarlet friend. Too bad Uncle Sam hasn't gotten Morgan Freeman or George Clooney to record the message....it would be so much more soothing....and, dare I say, sexy.

---

*This can vary from Camp to Camp

Fed Mart

Fed Mart

Fear not, you will be able to indulge in shopping while on sabbatical.

You can give your Neimans card a rest while you channel your inner bargain hunter/huntress.

Regardless of where you are residing there will be a Commissary (another US Government/Military term) locally known as Fed Mart.

The assortment of items varies depending upon who is running the store and their tastes. Of most concern is that there are no alcoholic products nor any potential products that could be used as a weapon or potential drug.

That being said, the selection is pretty amazing. From Nike running shoes to Dorito chips to MP3 players. You need not worry about any grey roots nor any stray hairs either, as there are ample choices in terms of hair coloring, perming and hair removal products.

You will be able to shop once a week and it is recommended that you arrive early as it can become quite a scene, especially when new items appear. Case in point, pints of ice cream sell out in the first hour.

The array of food products is all encompassing. Might I suggest that you get to know someone who is about to end their sabbatical so that you can learn some cooking tips and perhaps inherit their cooking tools (microwave bowls, utensils, etc.). There are two microwaves in each dorm as well as a hot water dispenser and a large industrial size ice machine (like the Marriott). These are also available 24/7.

Similar to your college dorm experience, you will be surrounded by smells of microwave popcorn and brownies every night.

Also reminiscent of your undergrad days, dining services becomes redundant. The menu is pretty consistent and you will get tired of eggs, chicken and hamburgers pretty quickly. Each Monday feels like Groundhog Day. You do not need to eat in the Communal Dining Room (CDR) at all, it's completely voluntary. Some people choose to not eat any meals there. That being said, during special occasions (e.g. Memorial Day, Christmas, etc.) they really go above and beyond with the amount of food and choices. You will not starve at Club Fed, quite the opposite, beware the carbs!

At Fed Mart you can purchase packaged tuna, chicken and vegetables as well as pasta and a wide array of spices. You have the potential to cook everything from Orange Chicken to Cheesecake.

For those WCCs with special dietary needs (soy allergies, vegetarians, etc.) you will find beans in every form available at almost every meal as well as accessible for purchase in Fed Mart. For the faddish Gluten Free among you, you'll need to man up and consume some Gluten.

In addition to the food choices there is an assortment of clothing available for purchase. Nike, Under Armour and Champion are the preferred brands. Work out shorts, pants, tops, sweatshirts, fleeces, socks, etc. You can even trade in your government issue black shoes and purchase Timberlands if you so choose. I'm not saying you won't miss Lululemon and RLX but you will be able to find what you need for your stay.

Prioritize your purchases. When you first arrive you will need your essentials (shower flip flops, extra towels, etc.). For WCCs your essentials might include some of the L'Oreal products on sale (e.g. eye cream) as well as the scented oils and thick cotton robes.

For women (and some WCC men) there is an array of facial products available for purchase. Facial scrubs, creams and makeup. Yes, there is foundation, mascara, blush and eyeshadow for the diehard among you! While Friends of F may be surprised at this expansive assortment (or as Aunt Cornelia would say "why the hell do you need makeup at Camp?") the theory is that by providing products and services to make people feel good about themselves it will lead to a more positive environment. Where do you think the expression "Happy Campers" comes from?

Scarlet Slippers

One can not stress enough how vital it is to procure a pair of flip flops as your first purchase upon entering Club Fed.

No, it's not to protect your manicured tootsies from heated tile floors.... nor is it to assist you in having tanned feet to avoid the unsightly tennis sock tan line.

No matter how much bleach is poured on the concrete floors or how clean you keep your living area, funky fungi abound at Club Fed.

Forget your 115mm Manolos and Choos (for the Ladies) and elegant Lobbs and Berlutis (for the Men)....your new shoe style of choice will include rubber soles and comfort is the goal.

Daytime footwear involves a thick rubber soled "practical" shoe....this could be Timberland (for Men AND Women) or a pleather black steel tipped style you probably have seen previously on your high school janitor. Depending upon your camp location you might even be provided with Docksiders boat shoes (flashback to summer sailing camp in Mystic!).

These shoes are given to you courtesy of Uncle Sam (another "thank you" to the American taxpayer). You can use your time in Fed Mart to purchase or special order a pair of Nike (or other named brand) running shoe for all of the physical activities available. This is highly recommended and, from a financial investment, a far better ROI than your spiked Louboutins!

In terms of flip flops, you will have a variety of options...from slides to traditional thong styles. Yes, those Adidas slides you see the Kardashians (and baes of Kardashians) wearing...you can also wear on your staycay. It is perhaps the only shoe that Rob Kardashian now sports for both day and evening...so, you are on trend!

Your newly purchased rubber flip flops should be coveted as if they were Dorothy's ruby slippers. From the shower to socializing, your new scarlet slippers will never be far away.

Post Fed Mart-yum Depression

Anticipation runs high prior to weekly shopping sprees while ensconced at Club Fed.

Will Fed Mart have replenished the perennially popular pop tarts? What new gooey chocolate items will be on display for purchase? Did new makeup palettes arrive? Have special order shoes been delivered? What about that waist trimming belt you have had your eye on?

While your Saks, Bergdorf and AMEX Black Cards take a rest at home while you are on sabbatical, one can still get their daily shopping dose at the Fed Mart on location.

Depending on where one is residing orders can be placed in person during shopping hours at Fed Mart or, in more secure facilities, orders may take place at a computer terminal and be delivered to you directly.

The assortment varies by location but there is normally a plethora of sweet and savory delights to quench dormant teen munchie desires in addition to an assortment of bath, body and hair products to enhance your beauty regimen.

Should one wish to improve their wardrobe there are clothing items as well, normally focused on athletic gear (running shoes, running shorts, jog bras, sweat shirts, athletic socks, headbands, etc.).

In terms of hobbies, there are crafty items (yarn and knitting needles), crossword books and a selection of cards to reflect the time of year and Hallmark holiday of choice.

You may (or may not) recognize many of the brand names, but it's best to forego the normal rigorous inspection process as the focus is less on quality and more on quantity.

What may be more surprising is less the excitement before shopping but the let down after shopping. Having spent their allotted one day a week of shopping and perusing a bag full of mediocre merchandise, sojourners lapse into a post Fed Mart-yum depression.

Perhaps it's from the cool down after the initial sugar rush or the guilt counting all of the calories consumed, but more realistic is the fact that you have to wait a full week for your next shopping "fix."

Club Activities

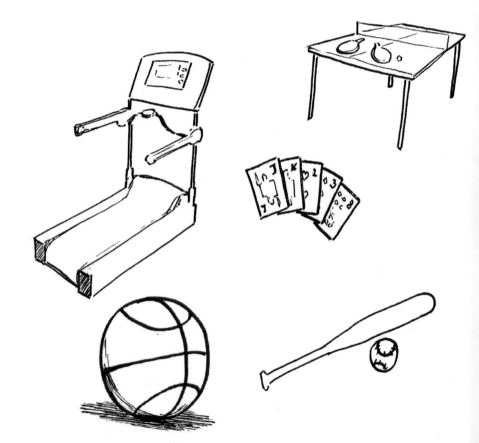

Softball, Spinning and Soccer Oh My!

Forget that Soul Cycle spin class you had to rush to after work to secure a seat for an hour of sweat and tears. You will have your choice of classes (Pilates anyone?) at all times of the day and night.

You can store your squash and tennis racquets as you will be trading them in for classes run by other WCCs. If you prefer an instructor led experience there are yoga, aerobics, step and boot camp (to name just a few) classes. If you would like to burn your calories privately you can jump onto one of the spin bikes, elliptical machines or treadmills to exercise away the carbs. Or if you enjoy group sports you can join the volleyball, softball or basketball teams. So many options. There is no excuse for you not to come home more toned than when you left.

Is it like training at Equinox? Sadly no, as there is no smoothie bar post workout nor steam rooms, but it's free (to you at least) and you don't have to be concerned about the way you look.

No need to worry about getting injured either as many of the volunteers (fellow WCCs) are chiropractors, MDs (an inordinately high number of podiatrists for some reason) and nurses. They are there, like you, to make the most of your experience by getting healthy and toned.

If you enjoy the outdoors, depending upon which Club Fed you are residing in, you can enjoy a run or walk on the pathways available.

Refer to the earlier information on Fed Mart for your wardrobe options. Sadly, Lululemon has not made it to Club Fed so you'll be saving a lot on matching your Nike IDs to your outfit as most items will be available in a limited color palette of 50 shades of grey.

If you are hankering for a taste of home, I recommend you put on your best white work out attire and grab three WCCs for a game of badminton with a cooler full of Arnold Palmers (Fed Mart iced tea mix combined with lemonade mix and a cup full of ice from the industrial sized ice maker in your dorm) for refreshment. Besides coolers, Fed Mart also sells a variety of water bottles and sweat bands as well as waist trimming/toning belts to round out your exercise gear.

If an ailment prevents you from partaking in the myriad of physical activities available to you, there are ample mental sports to occupy your time. Consider starting/joining a chess club. Not a Kasparov prodigy? How about Scrabble? Uno? All of the board games from your youth (and your parents) are available. Card games are also very popular. From classic (rummy, bridge) to regional (rook, spades). Take this time to fine tune your skills and learn new ones.

Camp Activities

Besides the myriad of athletic activities available to you at Camp you will find ample opportunities to engage other skill sets.

Should your stay be longer than a year you will be able to volunteer to train service dogs. Yes, Fido will live with you and you will be responsible for feeding, walking and training him/her until they are ready to go to a person in need.

Allergic to dander? Only visiting for a short period of time? How about teaching courses and assisting others in earning their GED. From rudimentary math and reading skills to essay and test taking preparation.

Is botany your thing? You could arrange elaborate flower beds on the extensive grounds or toil in the greenhouse cultivating plants to decorate Club Fed.

Looking to work up a sweat? Depending upon your location, there are vegetable gardens to plant. Homegrown tomatoes, corn and green beans all to be used by the kitchen to prepare meals.

If you fancy yourself a junior Bobby Flay or Ina Garten, try your hand in the industrial size kitchen whipping up lasagna or chocolate cake.

Prefer to get down and dirty? The maintenance crew are always looking for volunteers to fix clogs, paint or pour cement. If one so desires, and time permitting, they can earn a plumbing or electrical certificate for life after camp.

Fed U

Education is an oxymoron at Club Fed. The outdated facilities and materials make University of Phoenix look like Harvard.

Most WCCs have the advantage of a higher education but that doesn't mean your fellow Campers are operating at the same intellectual level. Those that do not have a GED will be required to enroll and attend classes while they are at Club Fed. This is a wonderful opportunity for those less fortunate to complete their degrees without any distractions. They literally have all day to study.

Should you wish, you can volunteer to teach. One should note that this is a thankless job as not all students are enthusiastic about being mandated to take GED classes.

Students range in age, background and ability. You might be surprised to see that a 56 year old can not pass a rudimentary math exam.

That being said, Uncle Sam is providing free educational opportunities to those that want to better themselves and there are those that have, for whatever reason, been unable to complete their studies and want to use their sabbatical wisely. It is for these individuals that you will gain the most satisfaction in your tutorial efforts.

Classes are diverse so you will be able to reflect back as you engage in algebraic variables and instruct in topics as diverse as "How to Balance a Check Book."

Muster every ounce of patience in your being and take this opportunity to give back. The rewards will be felt all around. The joy in seeing a student receive their GED under your tutelage will be better than any sports trophy on your mantle. Yes, even better than placing first in the Port Huron to Mackinac race!

Crafty Con
Thoughts of a glue gun send a tremor down your spine???

Have you bedazzled anything in your wardrobe?

Are you the first in line at a Michaels sale?

Do you have a vast array of wrapping paper in a multitude of hues to match the occasion (e.g. kelly green for St Patrick's Day, etc.)?

If you answered YES to any of the above questions you would be eligible to become part of the CCC also known as the Crafty Con Club.

Perhaps you are inspired by Martha Stewart's Club Fed sojourn and want to hand make all occasion cards and gifts?

Your creativity will be challenged and rewarded on sabbatical. With the limited resources available one needs to "think outside the compound" and make use of random items purchased at Fed Mart.

Purchasing some yarn and needles can lead to a bevy of beautiful items....monogramming your towels, creating a locker organizer, water bottle holder, blanket, poncho, stuffed animal, book bag, scarf, hat, booties...you name it!

Use the Uncle Sam sanctioned classes to your advantage....Beading 101 can produce bracelets, earrings and necklaces to use as gifts....Pottery 101 provides the resources to make mugs, bowls and decorative items for family and friends.

All you need is time (there is plenty of that) and the desire to create.

Perhaps after taking the Club Fed provided comic strip drawing class you can create a book of funnies for your daughter/son. No kids? Perhaps a series of more risqué comic strips for your friends to enjoy? Paper and colored pencils are in abundance...just look around....

You can learn the skills to become the next Jonathan Adler, John Derian or 21st Century Dorothy Draper!

If Gwyneth Paltrow can put together a collection of "must have" items on goop so too can you create a domain of desirables for your audience.

All you need is the desire to succeed and an open mind.

Club Privileges

Lavenderia

Thankfully laundry services are provided to you so no need to fret over having to wash and fold.

It might be good to brush up on your high school Spanish before you make the journey to Club Fed as most of the laundry services are run by Spanish speaking club members. If you become an amigo you can have your laundry washed and ironed to your specifications so that it is delivered to you still smelling of Bounce.

If you don't find that your khaki formals fit to your specifications you can also have your new friend tailor your clothes. The shirts and pants are notoriously loose fitting so if you want to highlight your newly toned body you can taper your shirts or pants.

All of these services come at a cost, so be sure your Fed Mart funds are sufficient to support these monthly expenses.

Your new BFF will also supply you with extra sheets, towels and blankets if you so desire. This comes in handy in the colder months.

As with your former tony Members Only Club back home there are cliques at Club Fed. It is important to be friendly with everyone, even if you don't socialize with them while on sabbatical, as they can be very helpful to you. For instance, when a new batch of clothing arrives you can easily exchange items with your contact in laundry or if you are friendly with someone in CDR you can get fresh fruit delivered to your room daily.

Fedkai

Concerned about split ends? No worries. Club Fed has a complete salon available to you, at no charge!

If you don't mind other WCCs practicing their newfound hair styling skills on you, you can get regular haircuts, hair color, perms, blow outs...whatever you so desire.

If you prefer to have additional services, or don't want to be a test dummy for someone getting their salon degree, find a WCC that managed a salon, or owned a chain of salons, that would gladly cut your hair (scissors are available for purchase in Fed Mart as are razors, shaving cream, hair removal cream, etc.) for a few treats from Fed Mart.

You will also have no problem finding people to provide manicures, pedicures and threading in exchange for a Fed Mart item. No need to look disheveled while on leave, especially if you are going to be utilizing Skype. Try to recreate a low budget version of Canyon Ranch.

In an attempt to recreate a spa environment, try rubbing some lavender oil on your temples at night and slather up your body with coconut oil. This treatment partnered with the fact that you are getting eight plus hours of sleep a night will take years off of you (which will make up for the years you aged during legal proceedings before you arrived at camp).

Styled by Club Fed

Now is the time to experiment while at your secluded retreat! Ever wanted to know what you'd look like with a new hair color/style?

In addition to the Clairol kits sold in Fed Mart, you can also purchase colored pencils and/or crayons which you can crush in a cup and add hot water to add a streak of pink, purple, etc. to your locks.

Better yet, purchase some Kool-Aid for a decidedly hip look...Oh Yeah!

On a budget or allergic to Clairol? Dilute some coffee grinds to cover your premature grays.

Cuticles in need of some TLC? Use coconut oil to smooth out the creases.

Has your skin become a bit dry due to the lack of daily Evian blasts...use some olive oil as a facial moisturizer.

Puffy eyes after an emotional phone call? Soak some tea bags and place over your eyelids.

Brows getting a little bushy? Find a friend who sews and can give you a good threading. If you prefer the old fashioned way, there are tweezers for purchase at Fed Mart that do the job.

Care to highlight the green in your eyes? Use the colored pencils sold in Fed Mart as eyeliner or if you prefer the smoky look smudge some of the darker shades under your eyes.

Desperate for some decent hair styling spray? Melt down some Jolly Ranchers in hot water..no joke...and put in a spray bottle...but beware, you may become a magnet for honey bees.

Try to recollect all of the styling tips you read about in Teen Vogue and recreate them at Club Fed.

No need to look disheveled or be a candidate for the Fashion Don't List.

Your new monastic wardrobe is bland enough, you need to contrast it with adding some color to your face and hair.

There are plenty of WCC's willing to assist you in creating your new Club Fed look. Unless you plan on utilizing Skype or having portraits taken during your staycay, experiment away!!

McDreary

Diehard WCCs are accustomed to stellar medical care from top rated physicians for treating everything from tennis elbow (the price one pays for a USTA rating of 5) to ghastly sun spots (from too many pre-SPF days at Siasconset Beach).

You will be taking a break from your diamond dust facials, laser treatments and teeth whitening appointments while at Club Fed.

Thankfully as a devoted WCC you have kept to a routine prescribed by your doctors of regular check ups and are in better than average good health.

The last thing you want to do at Club Fed is get sick, but if you do happen to chip a tooth (on candy corn from Fed Mart) or pull a muscle (practicing scorpion pose) don't expect McDreamy to come to your rescue.

More than likely the resident dentist will be sporting an ankle monitor and will specialize in extractions versus bonding and the "doctor" on call will not have an M.D. after their name but rather a series of initials unbeknownst to you that may or may not correlate to degrees.

Should you already be on medicine it will be provided to you. No expense is spared on dispensing pharmaceuticals to those in need. There are those that choose to sleep their way through camp by taking copious amounts of antidepressants which render them practically incoherent. Remember when Aunt Gwenyth was recovering from her second facelift and accidentally (?) took too many Vicodin? Yep, that type of incoherent drooling, sleep- inducing pills. This approach is not recommended for WCCs.

If your respite is less than a year it is recommended that you wait until you return home to have all of your annual check ups. Should your stay be longer, you will be provided with annual exams (dental, OB-GYN, etc.) courtesy of Uncle Sam.

It's best to avoid the daily medication cocktail (unless medically necessary) and channel your energy into getting mentally and physically fit. Some people manage to lose so much weight that they no longer need to take medicine for blood pressure or insulin for diabetes.

The underlying theme for WCCs is to manage this time successfully. As you have done with every other aspect of your life up until this point, set out a plan that you want to achieve and make it happen. Whether it is gaining the stamina to run a marathon, getting in touch with your inner animal spirits or simply reading every book/theory on JFK's assassination. Make it happen!

Are you there God, it's Me WCC

If you weren't overly religious before going to Club Fed, you will now have time to explore an array of religions.

Yes, in a an effort to be politically correct, Uncle Sam is providing you with every possible worship choice. From Wiccan to Judaism. There are even smoke lodge ceremonies if that floats your boat.

WCCs come from a fairly conservative background so the opportunity to learn about and further appreciate a variety of religions can be very liberating.

Ever sing in the shower? Now is your chance to try your hand at belting it out in the gospel choir. Shy about singing in public? Play a musical instrument in the church band.

Have an open mind. Break matzo with fellow campers over the holidays. Try fasting during Ramadan. Join in all of the various services (which are held weekly) and participation in celebrating religious holidays is welcome.

Every camp has an area devoted to worship as well as a Head Chaplain. Many have chapels that are open all day for you to pray, meditate, reflect or simply observe the various services.

Peace be with you. Shalom. Praise the Lord. Peace be upon you and the mercy of Allah.

And the Bride wore...khaki

No, Vera Wang has not signed a contract with Club Fed to design wedding gowns, nor has Monique Lhuillier lent her considerable talents to Uncle Sam.

Women (and Men) get hitched at Club Fed on a regular basis. The resident Chaplain may perform the ceremony or, given your religious affiliation, an appropriate religious figure can be secured to bind you in legal matrimony.

While your catering will be limited to the variety of treats available in the vending machines (apologies Mindy Weiss) and the guest list will be short, one can create an intimate environment to pledge your everlasting love.

One can even accept and wear a wedding band at Camp it just has to be all metal (sorry Neil Lane, no D Flawless stones allowed). Side note, earrings are also allowed (same caveat, no stones).

Perhaps hard to envision, given the years spent imagining your special day....peonies adorning your Preston Bailey designed floral arrangements, haute couture Oscar de la Renta rehearsal dinner attire, custom Manolo Blahnik Carolyne heels with your wedding date emblazoned inside....but Marcy Blum would be proud with the simple ceremony and, more importantly, the fact that two individuals commit to one another through such challenging circumstances.

Club Fed or....???

Club Fed or Club Med???

Before embarking on your journey to Club Fed, you may be pleasantly surprised to find the following similarities to Club Med......

Everyone arrives Single

You are located in a secluded/compound-like area

Food is all inclusive, as are activities

Everyone is on vacation from work/family

No cash is needed/accepted

Dress code is casual and comfy

Most are shy at first then, eventually, leap into the joint activities

You meet lots of new people from all types of backgrounds

For many it is their first time at club (and for those that are returning you can learn the ropes from them)

And finally.....

Similar to Club Med, what happens at Club Fed stays at Club Fed!!

Club Fed or Rest Home??

Club Fed bears a striking resemblance to your Nana's retirement home in Boca.....

Attire consists of:

> Elastic waist pants (maybe not en vogue but certainly comfy!)
> Comfortable/rubber soled shoes (more Wheezy than Yeezy)

Blended fabrics for easy wash/wear (did I mention water/fluid repellent?)

Dining options:

Weekly meal schedule (if it's Wednesday it must be burger day!)..changed semi-annually

Dinner at 5pm daily (gives you plenty of time to digest before 10pm lights out)

Special meals for holidays (New Year's, Fourth of July, etc.)

Lodging:

Antiseptic smell

Sheets cleaned weekly

Easy wash floors/walls

Activities include:

Board & card games (canasta anyone?)

Group exercise classes (step, yoga, pilates)

TV room with free cable

Music/Choir groups (most participants are tone deaf...or deaf in Nana's case)

All types of religious services provided

Medical attention:

Daily medical/pill line

Nurses on call 24/7

Dentist on-site

Transportation is provided between lodging and dining room (if needed/handicap)

Other commonalities:

> People bicker over TV channel choices
> Residents complain about minor things
> No cash/tipping allowed

Club Fed or Millennial Office??

How does your millennial approved office environment compare to Club Fed?

The similarities are endless....

- Hot water dispensers are available 24/7 to quench your thirst for hot beverages throughout the day

- Microwave ovens are available 24/7 to heat your morning gluten free breakfast, afternoon low calorie soup or evening organic snack

- Complimentary dining venue within easy walking distance from work space

- On site gym for afternoon stretch or after work/evening work out/class (no membership fee at Club Fed!)

- Gratis continuing education courses provided (should you wish to participate in them...highly recommended!)

- Comfortable temperature controlled environment

- Ability to go outside and eat on picnic benches or absorb some sun

- Co-workers are similarly attired in comfortable loose fitting clothes

- Plenty of space for an energizing walk or run (meet for ping pong or billiards game in the Rec?)

- Defined workspaces yet ability to roam and work outdoors

- Access to internal library/computer space

- TVs in gym and workspace (Uncle Sam even provides latest DVD released movies on weekends)

- Sports teams are formed and play together after work (Softball anyone? Volleyball? Take your pick)

- Volunteer opportunities are provided (Club Fed supplies yarn to produce blankets, toys, etc. for those in need. Club Fed also has training programs, at certain facilities, for volunteer firemen/women)

Need I say more? Uncle Sam has taken care of your every need at Club Fed....now, no excuses, make the most of your time away!

Fed Life

AKA

For WCC's you can't recall a time when you didn't have a nickname. Since birth your elder sibling has been known as Tripp, for the triple sticks after his name. You don't know your aunt by any other name than Bitsy and your pets even were known by names other than their given name.

Club Fed is much the same, though the names tend to be more descriptive.

Much of this has to do with the fact that you don't plan on forming lasting relationships during your stay nor can you recall everyone's name, hence the need to create a nick name that can easily identify the person.

Perhaps the rather masculine woman named Michelle is also known as MANchelle or the busty lady named Debbie that leads Step Class is otherwise known as Double D.

Rather than taking offense to a nickname, people wear them as a badge of honor. Some people will even take to introducing themselves with their Club Fed name.

It has been rumored that Martha Stewart's nickname at Camp Cupcake was M Stew which she enthusiastically accepted.

So embrace your temporary moniker and have some fun creating one for new sojourners.

Fraudulently Funny

You wouldn't think Club Fed was a place of great humor, but Second City should be spending more time with Uncle Sam to harvest the wealth of material available.

In your midst are an array of crimson characters that are full of scarlet sarcasm. These funny felons may not even be aware of the mirth they create.

While absorbing and translating the language of Club Fed a WCC will find amusing the interactions among the various groups of people. Whether it be chatter over playing cards or hilarious trash talking while cheering on your softball team, Amy Schumer has got nothing on these funny felons.

While waiting in line at Fed Mart a crimson crony may pop out of a large packing box startling you and setting everyone into fits of laughter. An otherwise mundane activity becomes amusing in your remote camp.

Think about the most basic skit on SNL that brought joyous tears to your eyes. A simple misunderstanding diffused with a raucous laugh. Who doesn't want to laugh or have fun? Even at Club Fed people want to smile.

It's not the land of the living dead, with the exception of those in a self imposed Prozac-induced zombie state.

Think back to your Boarding School days. Reach out to people, even if you are painfully shy. Try to find commonalities and find the joy that is all around you and just waiting to be tapped.

Wickedly witty opportunities abound. Lorne Michaels should hire some new "Players" that have been on sabbatical to add some much needed comedic talent to the new SNL cast.

When Kevin Hart jokes about his butt being a prison wallet to an auditorium full of people and their reaction shakes the roof, you know you have an abundance of gags at your disposal. You don't need to carry the Scarlet F to appreciate the humor gained at Club Fed

RSVP Not Necessary....Regrets Only

WCC's are accustomed to elaborate celebratory events, whether it be your annual birthday bash in the Bahamas, Thanksgiving with the entire extended family at the ski lodge or Christmas morning opening presents while sipping peppermint cocoa next to a roaring fireplace.

Should your staycay overlap with any of your special occasions, fear not. Your fellow camp mates are eager to organize a party. Never one to pass up a good invite, your weeks will be busy participating in birthday dinners, farewell brunches and attending various holiday celebrations.

It all starts with the food. Elaborate multi course meals, prepared meticulously, culminating in sweet desserts and gifts ranging from books to crocheted items.

Depending upon what Fed Mart has stocked for the week (and who you know that works in CDR), you might be indulging in a smorgasbord of lovingly prepared Spring Rolls, Chili Nachos, Chicken Fried Rice and Pepperoni Pizza followed by a dessert of Banana Bread Pudding, Oatmeal Raisin Cookies and Chocolate Lava Cake. Did I mention all homemade?! Yes, The Food Network has made it to Club Fed (in more ways than one).

WCC Hall of Famer Martha Stewart must have been impressed with the cooking techniques she witnessed while on sabbatical. Necessity is the mother of invention and the skill sets exhibited at Club Fed are truly worthy of Eagle Scout level praise.

Your fellow camp mates try to create a festive environment regardless of the circumstance. This might include hand crafted decorations and cards. If the weather is nice and an outdoor picnic has been organized you might find a bed sheet that has been stitched with whimsical motifs and used as a tablecloth. If you are participating in a pot luck brunch expect people to arrive with stacks of Tupperware overflowing with treats. If there is an artist in residence they might be doing caricatures during the event or a hair salon owner might be styling or braiding hair.

So, don't lose any sleep over missing out on entertaining while you are away from home...there will be plenty of opportunities!

The Scarlet Follies
If your sabbatical happens to coincide with a holiday be prepared for the Scarlet Follies.

Whether it's a crimson Christmas or a penal Passover, Club Fed and it's members know how to celebrate.

Planning a stay in December? Suffice it to say that Santa knows his way around Club Fed. Fed Mart prepares months in advance by stocking the shelves with criminally good peppermint cocoa, egg nog flavored treats and seasonal goodies (Peppermint flavored Oreos? *check* Candy Canes? *check* Cinnamon flavored Pop Tarts? *check*).

Carolling is organized so that those blessed (or not so blessed) with cherubic voices can belt out *Rudolph the Red Nosed Reindeer* and *White Christmas* while passing out holiday cookies and hot cocoa.

For the theatrically inclined there are opportunities to organize and perform plays/skits as well as a healthy competition among those on sabbatical as to the best productions, along with prizes.

Stockings are handed out as well! Mind the carbohydrates, for healthy options are limited. Treats lean more toward sinfully salty chips and corruptingly caloric candy bars, but who's counting?!

As you have a captive audience there is ample time to prepare for these events. Scarlet sisters might knit or crochet theatrical costumes and crimson cons can create choir robes from sheets.

Given the melting pot of professionals in your presence you could be delightfully surprised to find a designer, choreographer and opera singer that can put together a production to impress Joel (or Brad) Grey!

Not planning a visit in December but a summer sabbatical? Be prepared for July 4th cookouts complete with barbecue steak, angus burgers, baked beans, corn bread, coleslaw, corn on the cob, soda and ice cream.

After your feast you can compete in rigorous obstacle courses including sack races, bean bag toss competitions and hurdles, all designed by your fellow campers.

Teams prepare weeks in advance for the summer Scarlet Follies and are very selective in the screening process. Competition does not end at the entrance to Club Fed! You may even find professional sportsmen/women in your midst who offer to train you for the big day. Teams coordinate their outfits and it can be a great bonding experience creating a felon fraternity/scarlet sorority.

If you prefer mental exercises over physical there are bingo and card games you can join with prizes from Fed Mart. You might be pleasantly surprised at your elation over winning a bottle of perfumed lotion or a sleeve of soda to reward your efforts, a far cry from the sterling silver trophies on your mantle at home but cherished nonetheless.

Be prepared....Uncle Sam knows how to party!!

Crimson Christmas

The stockings are hung by the beds with care
While the smell of Fluff permeates the air
The peppermint cocoa is brewing
As the chocolate molten cake is cooling
The sounds of Christmas Carolling reverberates all around
As Holiday cards abound

Sound like home? Well, Club Fed can be a very festive place during the holidays.

Nothing compares to Nana's cooking or Aunt Edwina's special egg nog but Uncle Sam makes every effort to make your celebration away from home special.

A feast is prepared to rival the Last Supper with so many options your plate will be overflowing! Cornish hens, ham, mashed potatoes, green beans, corn bread....and the list goes on and on.....

The meal, events and gift of a candy stuffed stocking will take the sting out of being away from loved ones and appreciate them all the more.

Yes you will miss the flow of Veuve Clicquot, Aunt Barbara's truffled gravy and sweet potato pie and Cousin Michael's delicious Apple Pie but you will find joy in the simple pleasures at Club Fed.

Take the time to start planning your future holidays with loved ones after your sabbatical and making each moment extra special.

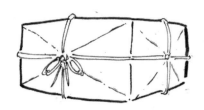

Friends and Family of F

Friends of F

The flashing F on your chest is a beacon that will either repulse people or draw your true friends closer.

No need to be a social pariah. You are still the same person inside, it's your new public persona that is Starbucks fodder.

Accept any invitation that comes your way. It's important for you and your family to keep life as normal as possible. Wallowing in self pity/regret is not helpful to anyone nor productive in the long run. You will soon find that more people have had run-ins with Uncle Sam than you ever knew. Perhaps they were just able to keep it a bit more on the down low, like when Daddy gave a big contribution to the local Police Department when Junior totaled his Jeep after the big football game after consuming a few too many brewskis.

While on sabbatical you can have visitors about 4 out of the 7 days and even more if a holiday week. This is an opportunity for you to put on your formal attire and greet your friends in the visiting room and indulge in the myriad of vending machine delicacies available to you while playing games or holding your spouse's hand.

Note to Friends of F: Don't keep asking "How are you?" As if your friend has a terminal disease. Ask them about their day, tell them about your day. Spending this precious time discussing "what ifs" or crying buckets of tears does no one good.

You will most likely notice a change in your WCCs appearance, of a positive note. WCCs get more sleep at camp. There are no 5am alarms getting you up and off for your commute to work. WCCs also have more time to read and actually digest a book/article as opposed to just skimming the headlines. They are open to having a real debate on a topic. WCCs also have a lot more time to exercise which means you will start seeing flatter stomachs and more toned arms and legs. Compliment your friend on their Club Fed glow.

If you want to treat your WCC to something nice, be the first to get to the vending machines with a pocket full of quarters to purchase a greek yogurt and cappuccino for your friend. Try to recreate the Saturday morning cafe experience you have enjoyed countless times in the past.

You will also be surprised to find that your WCC friend has made friends with fellow campers. Like the summer college campus programs your parents sent you to while you were in high school and they went on a European tour (ostensibly to prepare you for your SATs) WCCs meet people from all over the world and all backgrounds.

For the most part, campers are first time (non-violent) offenders. They've made a mistake and exercised poor judgement. Who can't relate to that? Campers share the same feelings of guilt, shame and remorse regardless of their backgrounds. That makes it a unifying experience.

That being said, your WCCs new friends may, at first glance, surprise you. Visible neck tattoos can be off-putting but try to have an open mind, as appearances can be deceiving.

Felon Family (FFs)

The Scarlet F extends beyond the individual. Families and Friends of Felons (FFs) are branded as well and feel the burden of knowing/being related to a WCC.

There is an audible gasp when FFs enter their country club or local restaurant. Heads turn followed by muted whispers. Invitations to parties and sports events decrease dramatically (social staples for WCCs). You can kiss the annual invite to your friend's suite at the Super Bowl goodbye. Same goes for the ski trip to Aspen and the summer folly in St Tropez.

Should an FF find themselves in a situation where they are engaged in polite cocktail conversation, initiate the inevitable question about your familial felon and provide a status report on your WCC, then immediately ask how THEIR family is doing. This diffuses the situation and addresses the elephant (or in this case WCC) in the room right away, thus avoiding any probing questions about your crimson crony.

Besides the murmurs and stares, family members that share the last name of the WCC find themselves in the unenviable position of having to explain their rouge relative.

A simple Google search will provide (sometimes inaccurate) details of their indiscretion. It is not up to FFs to defend their friend/family member but rather talk about what they are doing to support their wayward WCC. This will show FFs in the most sympathetic light and actually garner some much needed sympathy.

FFs need not fear being ostracized from society. Their compassion will be rewarded and the support they have given their WCC will be appreciated more than one can express in words.

The Virtues of Snail Mail
In our virtual world the art of hand written notes has been relegated to bygone times.

Given the absence of personal electronic devices at Club Fed you will yearn for your Mont Blanc fountain pen (that is lodged somewhere in the back of your desk drawer) and your Smythson monogrammed stationery.

Fear not carpal tunnel and start expressing your emotions in long hand versus emojis. You will soon find that there is a better way to express your feelings than smiley faces and swirly poop icons.

Mail Call is certainly one of the best parts of the day. It's when people gather Monday through Friday to eagerly hear their name called and rip open the cards and packages they receive.

Every word is devoured, every card savored.

There is a great silence that surrounds the dorm post Mail Call. People squirrel away to read sweet nothings, look at newly received photos and catch up on the latest political news (and, let's be honest, Kardashian gossip).

Friends of F are encouraged to dust off their stationery boxes and put pen to paper as your letters will be much appreciated at Club Fed, even if recounting your daily rituals.

Think back to when you were eagerly awaiting acknowledgement of your college applications and stared out the window waiting for the postman/woman to arrive....everyone knew a thin letter meant rejection and a thick letter represented acceptance.....in this case, ANY letter is joyfully received.

Instead of staring at a variety of LED screens at Club Fed you will be reconnecting with your cursive scripts and finding joy in the lost art of letter writing.

No one is expecting you to emerge as a reincarnated Twain, Joyce or Hemingway but you will find it refreshing to reawaken these lost skills.

Happy Writing!!

R & D

As mentioned previously, mail of all sorts is more than welcome when one is on sabbatical. That being said, the people who work in **R & D**, **R**eceiving & **D**elivery, can make obtaining the parcels challenging.

While mail is routinely examined for any unwelcome material (explicit pictures, edibles, etc.) and limits are put on the number of items that can be received daily (e.g. 5 magazines a day*) somehow, regardless of how closely one follows the rules, R & D will find a reason to return the much anticipated envelope.

Return & **D**eny is more accurate to describe the less than sympathetic processing of items sent from Friends of F.

Employees of R & D take pleasure in commenting on the pictures you send (they particularly get a chuckle out of scantily clad shots) and even

---

*Rules/Limits vary from location to location

partake in reading *People* and *US* magazines before they are passed along (note the smudged pages from Dorito dusted fingers).

Given the remote location and lack of higher education of the local employees, no need to fear them cracking open your *Architectural Digest* or *World of Interiors* subscriptions though...these will be safely forwarded....but if the mail delivery is particularly large on any given day, and the employees are anxious to get to their bowling league, you can be assured that whatever has not been examined will be returned with no reasoning provided.

Friends of F, be patient with returned mail, **R**e-direct & **D**ispatch.

For those on sabbatical, take a deep breath, **R**elax & **D**e-stress.

FAMILY OF F
You thought introducing your bi-racial transgender friend to your 100 yr old Grandmother was awkward...well, get ready to embrace the new addition to your family...The Scarlet F.

How do you introduce your wayward sibling/child/spouse when they return from their sabbatical?

When asked about their profession how do you respond?

When a new acquaintance Googles your last name and the first thing that pops up is an article on your tainted relation how do you handle the awkwardness?

In our Google-verse The Scarlet F effects the entire family, not just the one permanently labeled.

How one handles this new addition to the team is of paramount importance for all parties to proceed forward.

If you try to hide it, the tension will fester. Embrace it and you will begin to normalize.

That is not to say it won't be embarrassing, stressful and hurtful and that you won't have feelings of anger and betrayal. But, if you don't discuss this openly then no one can move forward.

The important thing is to remain a team. For better or worse you are connected, forever, so working together is far stronger than dealing with this alone. Not just for you, but for your Scarlet friend/family member. They need to know that the bond is strong in order for them to move forward and feel that they have a support system.

Once you broach the topic in an open manner people will then go through one or more stages of shock, revulsion and inquisitiveness but eventually realize that you, Family of F, are not to be blamed for your wayward relation and that you are your own person and should be heralded for being a supportive family member in a time of great need.

Yes, this is hard. To forgive is divine. No one is asking you to forget but to open your heart and show compassion and it will be returned many times over.

Family, forever.

Fed Up

Fed Up

It's not all peaches and cream at Club Fed. There are times when you are counting the days/hours/minutes until you are reunited with loved ones.

Don't let your frustrations get the better of you on your staycay. Like your annoying younger sibling you will find not all people on sabbatical are as industrious as you nor as pleasant.

Give the fact that you are all leading a rather unfulfilling, repetitive daily existence people tend to get bored, annoyed and testy.

Try to avoid those emitting negative vibes....the last thing you need while sojourning is someone greying your day.

Surround yourself with fellow WCCs and those that are taking the time to reflect, better themselves and others, improve/repair relationships and are making the most of their time at Club Fed.

If you find yourself in a situation where you are in a room of Pessimistic Patties/Peters make it clear that you are not interested in engaging in morose conversation or, better yet, excuse yourself and make note not to socialize with that group further.

Like your childhood Camp experiences, WCCs tend to gravitate toward fellow WCCs. It may take a little time, but you will settle into a clique.

Crimson Curmudgeon

We've all encountered the type at one point in our lives....the perennially bad tempered, negative opinioned person who specializes in bringing people down....

If you sense this Debbie/Doug Downer in your presence, RUN! You can almost hear the trombones playing WAH, WAH, WAH, as he/she approaches.

Unlike an SNL skit or Peanuts cartoon, this person is alive and living in your midst.

It's best to add this person to your Chuck It List and disassociate yourself from any future dealings.

Life is short, surround yourself with positive, active people that lift your spirits.

The old adage "positive things happen to positive people" is true.

Create and feed off of this uplifting energy. Seek continual improvement. Bad things do happen to good people, but the best people lift themselves up and move on to even better situations!

Scarlet Fever

Let's be clear, while Club Fed is an unplanned life break, and focused WCCs will attempt to make the most of their sojourn, that's not to say there will not be bouts of Scarlet Fever (SF).

Symptoms include longing for a hug from a loved one, FOMO on a child's special moment or not hearing your name called at Mail Call. SF can also be triggered by a letter received from a long lost friend or a missed phone call.

These symptoms can result in a pain in your chest, teary eyes or a desire to crawl into bed and hide under the covers.

The best treatment when aches of this type occur is to double down on your exercise...get those endorphins pumping....the aching in your heart should be from jumping rope or completing a 5k, not on missed scenarios.

Other treatments include watching a movie (preferably a comedy) in the Library from the DVD assortment available or reading an engaging novel (perhaps Walt Disney's biography).

It is imperative that you do not stay in bed. The prescription is for movement and interaction.

If one does happen to succumb to SF and lay down in bed for a pro-longed period it could escalate to SD (Scarlet Depression). One wants to avoid this at all costs as it could lead to weight loss/gain and a need for prescription medicine.

SF can be contagious. It is best to avoid those that are suffering from this condition as it can spread very rapidly.

Once you have experienced SF it can recur so it's best to be aware of the symptoms so as to be able to address them immediately.

Fed-tastic!

Staying positive and focused on making the most of your sabbatical to Club Fed is of paramount importance.

How do you turn that frown upside down? Dig deep and don't waste time....time flies when you are having fun....so amuse yourself.

Get creative....and I don't mean artistic (unless this tickles your fancy).

Think back to those rainy days at your family's cabin in Maine, pre-Apple TV, when the board games were dusted off and your slightly tipsy uncle initiated a game of charades.

Don't wait for (or expect) others to entertain you. While there is no doubt the 'people watching' aspect of time spent at Club Fed is better than any Bravo TV show episode, by engaging in activities and creating new opportunities one will not only be occupying their brain, but also their body.

Clearly, it's up to the individual as to how they want to pass their time during their time at Club Fed, but mind the mantra that a "Healthy Body Equals a Healthy Mind" and vice versa.

Stay active! Stay positive!

Scarlet Survival

LexiCON

Get ready to expand your vocabulary at Club Fed. You may learn a few new words that haven't made it to the OED (yet).

Bulldagging

Girl on girl action, need I say more?

Call Out

Mon-Fri a "Call Out" sheet is delivered along with the mail. This sheet lists all of the various classes, programs, medical appointments, etc. for everyone at Club Fed. You should review this list daily to see if your name appears so that you aware of any designated engagements and adjust your schedule accordingly.

CDR

Acronym for Communal Dining Room. Similar to your Marriott catered college meal plan. Serving 3 meals daily, buffet style. Attendance is optional. Formal attire required for breakfast/lunch weekdays. Casual attire when eating dinner and on weekends.

Commissary

Federal/Military term used to describe the on site grocery/clothing/cosmetic store. Normally open 5 days a week but shopping time may be limited based on size and staffing of store. Locally known as Fed Mart.

Con Air

Transfers of camp mates via Federal airlines. For those that can not drive themselves to camp, they can be transferred courtesy of Uncle Sam on federally supplied transportation. This is not recommended as you could be sitting next to someone that is scheduled to go to another higher security facility. The seats and food are also not up to Business Class standards, to put it mildly.

Cop Out Sheet

Should you wish to make an appointment at Cosmo, sign up for a class in Education, etc. you need to complete a form called a Cop Out Sheet and drop it off at the respective mailbox. It will be returned to you with a reply (at Mail Call) normally within a few days.

Cosmo

Club Fed has a full service cosmetology facility (locally known as Cosmo) where you can schedule an appointment for a hair cut, hair color, manicure, etc. Disclaimer: these services are performed by fellow campers. One can apply to earn a Cosmetology degree if their staycay is longer than 3 years. During this time you will learn, through study and practical experience, and eventually earn a Cosmetology degree.

Cottage Maintenance

A lovely way to describe those that work cleaning the dorms. A realtor must have come up with this glamorized term for a rather dirty job. This involves the cleaning of the bathrooms, showers, common areas (TV room, ice dispenser, etc.) in preparation for weekly health inspections. The dorms are rated by cleanliness and those with higher levels get preference in attending CDR.

Counts

Several times a day you will be required to check in to be counted. This is to ensure that no one wandered off campus. Nothing is required of you but patience. Times vary depending upon which Club Fed you are attending but assume one in the morning and one in the evening.

County

Club Fed is your temporary home away from home with basic amenities. County is a local holding facility that is more akin to where one would house a stray rabid animal. You will be sent to County if you get shots or take an extended trek off campus. Unless you are interested in having a Guantanemo experience it is recommended that you adhere to all of the Club Fed rules.

Dog Program

Should your sabbatical be of a substantial length (2 plus years) you would be eligible to apply to train dogs for people in need. This requires you to have the dog live with you and you would be responsible for feeding, walking, training, etc. Dogs can vary in size and temperament so this is recommended for people who consider themselves dog whisperers.

Education

There are a variety of educational programs available to you during your stay at Club Fed. From the basic (Balancing a Check Book) to the more advanced (Starting a Business). In order to pass your time productively it is highly recommended that you participate in some of the courses to avoid boredom. Better yet, try your hand at teaching a few if you are so inclined.

FCI

Acronym for Federal Correctional Institute. Another low security institution (FPC is the lowest). A more defined perimeter (double fencing) and higher staff to sojourner ratio.

FPC

Acronym for Federal Prison Camp. A minimum security institution with little or no perimeter fencing and very low staff to sojourner ratio. Sometimes referred to locally as Camp Cupcake. Primarily first time non-violent offenders (lots of WCCs!) in your midst.

Firefighter Training

If you are taking an extended staycay (say 3 plus years) you can apply to be accepted into a program to train to be a firefighter. Candidates should be strong (ala Ronda Rousey or John Cena) as you will be participating in timed drills and need to be agile enough to carry heavy equipment. If agreed upon with the local community, you may be called to assist in fighting fires outside of your Camp, otherwise you will be relegated to dealing with only issues on site.

HWH

Acronym for Half Way House. When departing Club Fed some people enter these facilities before returning home. Unlike Club Fed where Uncle Sam paid for your stay, at the HWH you must pay for your stay. Rules are pretty much the same, so it is suggested you avoid this scenario as the HWH's are normally in very bad areas and it's best to stay at Club Fed and go directly home.

Horticulture

Certain Camps have greenhouses where you can learn how to grow plants, vegetables and herbs (of the therapeutic kind). While most of the time is spent tending to decorative plants around your retreat, you can also volunteer to work the more laborious vegetable gardens where food is grown for CDR. The benefit is that you can use the herbs to make fresh mint tea or spice up your cooking, if you so desire.

HSU

Health Services Unit. This is where you would go for any medical issues and to pick up any prescriptions/medications. Equipment (and staff) are outdated and not recommended unless you are truly sick/injured.

inmate.com

Fellow campers are eager to share information they hear as they are deprived of their daily tweets, news alerts, etc. Word to the wise...always double check (and in this instance, triple check) what you hear.

Laundry

Fairly self explanatory. This is where you drop off/pick up your laundry weekly. Sheets, blankets, clothing, etc. will all be laundered. For a minimal monthly Fed Mart fee you can contract with an employee of Laundry to do this for you and return freshly laundered and folded/ironed clothes directly to your room. Should you also require different clothes this is where you would exchange/pick up shirts, underwear, pants, coats, etc. as well as tailored items.

Library

A repository of books for your reading pleasure normally open 7 days a week. In addition to the plethora of romance novels you can also find the latest magazines (*Time* to *Town & Country*) and an entire collection of encyclopedias. Since internet access is not permitted at Club Fed take this time to unplug and re-read some classics or explore Stephen King's twisted stories.

Mail Call

Yes, mail is delivered to you Mon-Fri. In addition to USPS, most camps also receive UPS and Fed Ex shipments daily. It is normally delivered in the early afternoon and will be distributed 2-3 times a day. Your name will be called in your dorm and you can pick up the cards and books/magazines sent from Friends of F. If you were sent a package with unapproved contents (e.g. brownies) you will need to go to the Mail Room and pay to have it returned or discarded.

Mail Room

A separate area/building where all of the mail is processed. This is where you would go to ship packages (crochet blankets, Fed Mart purchases for your children, etc.). For basic letters there are mailboxes around Club Fed where you can drop your letters/cards. Stamps (and cards) can be purchased at Fed Mart.

Perc

This is short for Percoset, a drug. Any number following normally refers to the dosage.

Pill Line

Set time(s) daily for one to pick up medication. Normally ingested as received

Pillow Princess

One that enjoys bulldagging.

Quiet Time

On the weekend, it is requested that noise is kept to a minimum in the early morning hours. This is to everyone's benefit, to allow for people to sleep in (if they so desire), relax, etc. Counts are delayed on the weekends but all of the other facilities are open (Rec, TV Room, etc.)

Rec

The recreation center is a beehive of activity. From those who are using the fitness machines (elliptical, treadmills, etc.) to those participating in group exercise classes (yoga, step, pilates, etc.) to those playing or watching sports teams (basketball, volleyball, etc.). Depending upon your camp, there could also be a stage for theatrical performances, tables and chairs for playing card/board games, and lots of TVs for watching news, etc. while enjoying the benefits of Rec.

ROY

Rumor on the Yard. Similar to Inmate.com, information shared freely that may or may not be accurate.

RDAP

Residential Drug Addiction Program. This is not available at all Camps but should you have a drug related issue you can apply for admission. RDAP participants live in a separate dorm all together and adhere to a stricter set of rules. Classes are held daily and participation is mandatory. Should you successfully complete the program you will be eligible to leave Club Fed early.

Shot

No, not with a syringe. A "Shot" refers to something you have done wrong. A better term would be black mark. It's the opposite of a gold star. The more shots you get, the more severe the punishment. You want to avoid shots at all costs. A minor shot might entail one having to do some menial cleaning task. A more severe shot could result in you being moved off campus.

Sick Call

Normally early in the morning and limited number of days per week at HSU. This is where you would go to wait to be seen for minor issues (cold, toothache, etc.). If you have a more serious illness (broken arm/leg, etc.) you will be taken to a local area hospital and treated.

Visitor Room/Center

Yes, you can have visitors at Club Fed. On average, about 4 days a week and about 6 hours a day. The Visitor Room is full of tables and chairs and, weather permitting, there are also tables and chairs outdoors for you to sit, walk, talk, etc. For the children there is a playroom and, depending upon the camp, outdoors activities (swings, etc.). No, there is nothing separating you, you can hold hands, hug, kiss, etc.

Yarn Project

If you can knit/crochet this is a wonderful program to participate in. Yarn is provided to you to make items to be sent to the needy. Children's blankets and toys as well as bed blankets are being churned out weekly by fellow Campers.

Straight at the Gate...and Back

For some reason, everyone seems obsessed with the question about sex at camp. College fantasies run rampant in people's minds. Not to put water on your fire, but Club Fed is not Club Med.

Inside every woman does not rage a lascivious lesbian nor does every man have images of English boarding schools running through his head (not familiar with Eton and the like? Watch *Another Country* on Netflix).

First off, camps are single sex environments where you are more likely to hear people speak longingly for their families and friends.

Secondly, this is hardly the time to experiment. While you are surrounded by primarily first time non-violent offenders, many of these people were drug users/abusers and might even be taking antivirals in their daily medical cocktail.

How does one feel sexy in 50 shades of Champion grey, even with the most flattering tailoring? If the external contractor fixing the leaking sink starts looking attractive to you...take a cold shower.

If people are "Gay for the Stay" they were gay before the stay. You don't change your sexual preference over night. If you are gay and wish to meet someone there are ample opportunities. It's like one giant same sex mixer so have your pick. Those that are gay and unattached will make themselves known. Even someone without gaydar can easily pick out the resident Lesbian (crew cut, low slung pants, mannish walk) or Fag Stag.

Did Someone Say Shots??

When you get a shot at Camp it's not like when Uncle Clifford bagged a pheasant during your trip to South Dakota, nor is it like the booster shot the nurse gave you before safari with the family to celebrate Pop Pop's 80th.

A shot at Camp means you have run afoul of the rules. Yes, there are rules at camp. Very basic and easy to adhere to, so try to read your welcome manual so that you don't end up getting a shot.

No, there are no bullets involved. No one has a gun at camp.

A minor shot means you have done something silly like miss a count.

A more severe shot for, let's say, making sloe gin, could result in you losing the right to have visitors or not being able to purchase anything in Fed Mart.

As WCC's need their weekly retail therapy it is not recommended that you ignore the code of conduct, even if you were trying to recreate an afternoon at Raffles sipping Singapore Slings.

Given this generation's dependence on all things electronic, some people obtain cell phones while on break. Not only is this not necessary, as you have access to phones about 18 hours a day, but it's a rule breaker. This type of no-no would result in a severe shot and one could even end up being sent to County.

Gasp.

Yes, County is an ugly word. This means you would be transferred from Camp Cupcake to a really dingy holding center in your local rural town where you might be fed a bologna sandwich. Gag. Unless you are interested in recreating a scene from *Misery* with Kathy Bates as your room mate it is strongly recommended that you abide by the simple rules set forth.

The Scarlet Underground

If you can't embrace the clean living at Club Fed and truly can't forego your electronic devices nor your nicotine and adult beverage cravings then there are options for you to obtain these amenities.

Let's begin with the basics. Just like when you were trying to pass as 21 and your 18 yr old baby face wouldn't get you the beers you needed to host a homecoming bash, all you needed to obtain the party essentials was a few extra bucks to your college age neighbor home on break.

While no hard cash is allowed at Club Fed, you do have access to a bank account whereby you can purchase items at Fed Mart such as food, clothing, photo cards, etc. to offer in exchange for non camp approved fare.

If no cash is available to you there are other ways to barter for the items you are jonesing for...the industrious will offer to iron clothes, clean living spaces, carry Fed Mart purchases, cut hair, give manicures/pedicures and cook for you.

If you crave more than your daily allotment of fresh fruit then become friendly with someone that works in CDR that can bring you the oranges you need to make fresh squeezed orange juice daily....better yet, a Mimosa with the homemade hooch your camp mate fermented with potatoes he/she saved.

In need of some Marlboros pronto? Just start sniffing around and follow the nicotine trail...you will find surprisingly well wrapped fags. Need a light? Your friend who works in maintenance has access to all types of tools to provide a spark.

Tired of tearing out the magazine samples as your source of personal fragrance? Fed Mart has started selling body washes that can provide you with the perfumed air you so desire. This varies from site to site but there is normally one choice that has some type of scent (fruit, flower, musk). If you prefer something more organic ask your friend in Lawn Maintenance for some of the mint or rosemary they are growing on the property.

Aching to call your significant other (SO) in the middle of the night? Cell phones can be procured by multiple means. The daring will smuggle one in during a visit or have one left near camp that can be picked up. With the invention of drones the possibilities are now limitless.

In the mood for something more naughty? People in Horticulture are growing more than jade plants....and people will grind up just about anything they can snort.

The ingenuity demonstrated at Club Fed would have impressed Harriet Tubman but keep in mind that any of these actions can result in a shot.

Scarlet F 2.0

Initially branded with the Flashing F (for Felon), you can now proudly respond to inquiries as to the new meaning of the Crimson Character F:

Free
Fearless
Friendly
Fun
Forgiving
Faithful
Fit
Flexible
Focused
Forward Thinking

First and Foremost, Focused on living a Fulfilling life!!!

A Brave New World

Upon completion of your sabbatical one could easily flip the page on your sojourn and leave Club Fed in your distant past.

While one should not dwell on the experience, your time at Club Fed can not be erased from your personal resume so you might as well embrace it and become a scarlet supporter and fear not the embarrassment of your blazing F.

As daunting as the prospects may be, one can not look back, one must surge forward.

Do not feel the need to be labeled an Epsilon. You can become an Alpha now that you are removed from your Uncle Sam controlled environment.

Unlike Huxley's tragic tale, you can create a new destiny and not fall prey to life's enticements.

Staying focused and positive is the key to life after Club Fed. Don't succumb to the naysayers!!

Fortuitous Felons

How can it be that those bearing the Scarlet F are fortunate?

They are fortunate for the perspective they have been provided. Uncle Sam has given them the time and opportunity to improve themselves, away from their daily distractions. By stepping out of their comfortable environment, Club Fed has made WCCs more compassionate and more appreciative of the people and things around them.

Did a WCC ever imagine that they would befriend a disbarred lawyer at Club Fed or a drug dealer? Did it ever cross their mind that they would be swapping microwave recipes with someone named T-Rex? Or being the only straight white person on an all gay black basketball team?

Time apart from loved ones may be difficult, but the time away allows a WCC to re-evaluate those that matter in their lives and the people that they want to continue to partner with on their journey through life.

While working non-stop a WCC never had the chance to really sit back and analyze the direction they were tumbling toward at full speed. Days, weeks, months, YEARS flew by and before they knew it they were getting invites to their prep school's 25th reunion!

Club Fed is a unique sabbatical in that a WCC is removed from all distractions (okay, maybe not all, but certainly most) and all luxuries (definitely all luxuries!). People pay top dollar to go to an Aman resort to escape and re-boot, at Club Fed Uncle Sam is footing the bill. Take advantage of this rare opportunity.

Fearless Felon

Remember the NEW meaning of the Scarlet F. You need to be **F**earless in pursuit of your new goals. Do not shy away from the unknown. Surge forward and capture all that life has to offer.

The only person holding you back is you.

Yes, life can be difficult, especially after Club Fed, but start Fresh and Find your new passion. Don't get lethargic, don't succumb to depression, Fight off any negativity and Focus on this next chapter of your life.

This may mean not only thinking differently, but also acting and living differently. Re-assess the most important aspects of your life.

Yes, yachting off the coast of Monaco is divine, but is it really essential to living a Fulfilling life?

Tasting the latest Tom Keller concoction may be delicious, but can't you improve your kitchen skills and create something tasty?

Gain a new appreciation for the people and things around you. You will begin to see things differently. Be a good Friend, be a good employee, be a better person.

Do not look back...propel yourself Forward.

Simply Scarlet
With your new Scarlet status don't expect people to be fawning over you as they may have before. Expect people to have little sympathy for you and your situation. After all, YOU did create your current situation. Time to accept responsibility and move forward.

Those that continue to blame others and wallow in a "woe is me" attitude will never move forward nor will they ever achieve success in their second act of life.

No need to exile yourself Ivan Boesky-like.

Simply do as you have always done....work hard and stay focused and positive.

Those who set goals for themselves (and meet them!) will succeed.

Prove to everyone that you can be successful again and that you don't want to be remembered for one error in an otherwise stellar life/career.

F Marks the Spot

Upon completion of your sabbatical, having read every Booker Prize recipient and NYT Best seller, mastered a second, third or fourth language, lowered your blood pressure by 20 points and slept more than you have since incubating in your Mother's womb, you are ready to tackle your biggest challenge to date....employment.

You can't exactly update your Linked In account with Club Fed details, nor will you be able to complete any employment contracts without answering a question about The Scarlet F.

Your best course of action is to embrace your new status. Wear it like a badge of honor. Many will be curious about your staycay, use this to your advantage in engaging people in conversation that could lead to an assignment.

You have already taken responsibility for your actions, presumably made amends and expressed great remorse. Now is not the time to wallow in self pity. Now is the time to surge forward with phase 2 of your life.

Is there something you have always wanted to do/explore as a career? Perhaps you want to develop your cooking skills? The Food Industry is accepting of applicants with The Scarlet F.

Thoughts of the kitchen repulse you? What about using your hands in construction? There are positions in back office as well as "on the ground" opportunities.

Food and construction Industries aside, consider starting your own business.

WCC's are not content to sit back and relax. Why not explore an opportunity that germinated during your many hours of contemplation.

Make it a reality. Put together a business plan and discuss with your trusted colleagues.

The reality is that The Scarlet F severely limits one's ability to obtain a traditional WCC position. Regardless of whether or not you need to "check the box" on an employment application, a basic googling of your name or background check will bring up your history. It's best to be up front and honest.

Given this fact, WCC's need to be creative in repackaging themselves and forthcoming in assessing their strengths and weaknesses.

Perhaps the years of sailing and tennis lessons could lead one to organize a youth sports training program?

Self employment is a great avenue. You are your own boss (no box to check), you can utilize your own resources or you can partner with trusted family members/friends in growing a concept to fruition.

Be realistic. If your idea of job security is creating a reality show and you envision yourself a star on the E! Network then your prescription dose needs to be re-evaluated.

Scarlet Supporters (Friendlies)

Outside of Friends of F there are also corporations supportive of the crimson.

A simple query will reveal those businesses that have 'banned the box' or welcome former members of Club Fed.

Many opportunities reside in the hospitality and construction industries and, thinking outside of the box:

Dave's Killer Breads
daveskillerbread.com

It's Founder, Dave Dahl (a crimson crony), started the company in 2005 and it was acquired by Flower Foods in 2015 for $275 million. If you want to become a Breadhead contact the Oregon based company.

Greyston Bakery
www.greyston.org

Since 1982 Greyson has provided employment to those in need. They are based in Yonkers, New York and are Scarlet Supporters.

Prison Bars
http://prison-bars.com

Seth Sundberg, a former NBA player (and a Scarlet F bearer), started this company that makes healthy granola bars. Based in San Francisco at 1859 Powell Street (#213). They can be reached at (415) 964-0675.

Underground Coffee
undergroundcoffeeproject.com
undergroundcoffee@newearthworks.org

Founded in 2007 by jail chaplains and a few former inmates and addicts (located at 102 North Pine Street in Burlington, WA 98233). Provides job opportunities for ex-offenders (interested in coffee roasting?) also associated with Hidalgo Bay Coffee Roasters at 856 North Hill Blvd in Burlington, WA (98233), Hidalgobaycoffee.com.

Together We Bake
togetherwebake.org
@togetherwebake

Founded in 2012 they provide an empowerment based job training program for women in need of a second chance. Located in the Washington DC area.

The Lancaster Food Company
www.thelancasterfoodcompany.com

@landcasterfoodco

Established in 2014, this organic food business is based at 341 East Liberty Street in Lancaster, PA 17602 and currently produces bread and maple syrup with the goal to expand into other products. Contact this crimson crony at (717) 508-7268 to discuss opportunities.

Other sources include:
secondchancejobsforfelons.com

Nonpartisan Support

After childhood camp expeditions you were eager to share your experiences while being inundated with questions from your friends and family who wanted to hear all about your escapades. Your interactions post Club Fed will be markedly different.

Polite people will shy away from asking about your time apart. Those that lack good manners will be less subtle and the acquaintances that have been Grey Goose Martini inspired will make particularly inappropriate remarks, but for the most part, people will not pry about your sabbatical.

Friends of F only knowledge of Club Fed is based upon MSNBC TV shows highlighting the most intense environments which tend to be poorly maintained and managed and lacking in civilized colleagues and interactions.

In an effort to put your friends and family at ease you should feel free to share snippets of your Club Fed sojourn. Keep in mind that not everyone wants to hear about this episode in your life so know your audience before launching into a story about your participation in Club Fed.

Where your prepubescent and adult bivouac involvement will be similar is that you will form unexpected friendships with people from a variety of social circumstances. People tend to gravitate toward those that share/exude the same milieu but their sphere may expand due to curiosity and their exposure to divergent personalities.

Exposure to disparate people can be eye opening/liberating. Unconventional relationships can form which continue after Camp. The bonding that occurs is based upon your shared trials and tribulations and, of course, The Scarlet F.

Friends of F should not shun these new additions to your circle, but realize they are no different than your lifelong friend and simply participated in a shared furlough, not unlike the many vacations you have taken to exotic locales.

CONnected
If you thought you had a powerful social network before sabbatical get prepared for an entirely new spectrum of associates.

Bonds formed at Club Fed are stronger than those fostered over years of social gatherings and activities. This includes the vows taken at your clandestine Ivy League club or the inseverable Greek ties formed at your fraternity/sorority.

You will be able to share your inner most feelings, your doubts, your insecurities, your jubilations with those fellow sojourners who you shared this precious time with without fear of repercussion.

While it may be difficult to explain or comprehend, Club Fedmates are like swans...they stay committed for life.

Prior to attending Camp you will find this incomprehensible but once you have shared this special time together you will morph into a swan.

Crimson Crony
How does one introduce their new scarlet sister or fraternal felon?

The Scarlet F is not branded on one's head nor is it emblazoned on one's shirt pocket.

"I'd like to introduce you to Donna, we met at (fill in the Club Fed blank)"....not exactly like your previous introductions...."Bitsy and I met on holiday in Capri while snorkeling in the Blue Grotto"...

Assuming your new crimson crony doesn't have a shotgun tattooed on their face, there is no need to feel awkward about introducing your campmate to friends and family.

Sometimes the bonds formed on sabbatical are an experience shared that can't compare to prior social engagements.

Good people are good people regardless of any mistakes they may have made. In many cases they are "re-born" during their sabbatical and lead very productive/positive lives.

Need some examples? Would you introduce a musical friend to Jay Z? How about a die hard Conservative to Dinesh D'Souza? A celebrity columnist to Robert Downey Jr? All are bearers of The Scarlet F and all have become more successful AFTER attending Club Fed.

Perhaps adding Club Fed to your social profile has a positive effect and meeting your new crimson crony could be a bonus in a social gathering? If anything, it makes for interesting conversation!

If Emily Post were alive today she might recommend that you address any initial awkwardness by asking your crimson crony how they would like to be introduced then follow their lead.

Chuck It List

You made it this far, now get ready for the real challenge. The Real World can be an ugly place.

The Scarlet F is going to be with you forever so just come to terms with it or you'll just frustrate yourself further.

You thought the shame, embarrassment and self flagellation ended before camp? Get ready to re-enter society as a social pariah.

You will need to channel your inner Gloria Gaynor and surge forward. This is your time to reinvent yourself, version 2.0.

Things will not be the same, no matter how much you try, and that's okay.

In your heart you know you are the same loving person as before, but people will view you differently. Don't spend your time trying to convince them you are the same person they adored prior to your staycay, just focus on spending time with the people that make *you* feel good.

If people feel awkward around you then that is an issue they need to resolve. If your mother suggests that you shouldn't wear a horizontal striped top because it might remind people that you were at camp just laugh it off.

Note: No striped clothes are provided to you. You are surrounded by a sea of khaki and grey. You will be craving patterns of any kind when you depart.

Use this experience as a stepping stone to your new career. Start your own business, go back to school and get a new degree, counsel others going through a similar situation, do something you never thought you would have time to do....start a Chuck It List.

That's right...Chuck It. As opposed to a Bucket List of items that you want to do before you die, a Chuck It List is a list of things you should remove from your life that are not constructive. This is not limited to objects or experiences, but also people.

If you have negative influences in your life you should make every effort to distance yourself from them. This could be a childhood friend, former co-worker or even a family member. It could also be a favorite food, beverage or activity (like smoking) that you previously didn't think you could function without but now realize, having been Taittinger, Dunhill and Cadbury free during your staycay, that you can manage without.

Don't fall back into former bad habits. If you have been exercising 1-2 hours a day during your sabbatical, maintain that pace post camp. If you learned a new language at Club Fed, continue practicing it and perhaps even take it to the next level.

If anything hinders you from achieving a happy and healthy life... CHUCK IT!

Fed EX

As a tried and true WCC you have most likely been in at least one committed relationship throughout your life. You may or may not be currently married but you are traditional in the sense that you believe in one partner (at a time) and marriage.

Well, at Club Fed you are going to come into contact with sojourners that do not share your background/beliefs.

You will hear camp mates refer to their significant others as "baby momma"/"baby daddy" as opposed to husband/wife. They may also have more than one baby momma/daddy. While this term is rather self explanatory it is indicative of the era in which we live. People are not necessarily committed to their significant others (SOs) and here are some telltale signs to think about when you complete your sabbatical and re-enter life with The Scarlet F.

If your SO does any of the following he/she has lost that loving feeling toward you:

-Your "date night" consists of the two of you eating at the bar (versus the lovely tables nearby) as your SO chats with the bartender on a first name basis.

-Your SO has acquired all of your pre-sabbatical closet, drawer and medicine cabinet space.

-Instead of referring to the two of you as "we" it's now "me" or "you."

-When your SO introduces you to new friends/acquaintances you are referred to by your first name as opposed to "my partner/SO/wife/husband."

-Special dates (Birthdays, Anniversaries, Holidays) are not jointly celebrated or simply forgotten/shrugged off.

I know, it seems rather obvious when observing from afar but when people are emotionally wrapped up in their SO they tend not to notice the glaring signs or make excuses for them, so hopefully a Friend of F will read this and take them aside to explain the painfully evident.

It is at this point that you should relegate this former SO to your Chuck It List. Life is difficult enough post camp so it is necessary to be surrounded by (and supported by) those that value you.

Repeat Offender
One would think that one trip to Club Fed was enough but you might be surprised to hear that there are those that return!

Is it the college cafeteria inspired food? Perhaps a RO didn't like cooking at home and prefers to be have three meals a day prepared for them?

Is it the monochrome uniform? Perhaps a RO didn't like spending time coordinating colorful outfits and doing their own laundry?

Is it the convivial dorm setting? Perhaps a RO missed the comradery that comes in a communal living environment?

Whatever the reason, people do return to Club Fed, normally because they could not abide by the rules post sabbatical. These crimson culprits are not only doing a disservice to themselves, but also to their families and friends.

You can tell an RO because when they arrive at Club Fed they are greeted with high fives by fellow sojourners and quickly adapt to their familiar surroundings.

What would propel someone to return to Club Fed? Can things be that bad at home? More than likely an ex-Fedmate has returned to familiar surroundings and habits and has not used their sojourn to improve their situation.

Violators, as they are known to Uncle Sam, have not abided by the terms of their probation.

What is so difficult about following a few rules? Why add to your Scarlet resume?

While it is challenging to find employment with the Scarlet F, one should not get discouraged.

Many industries are "banning the box" and working toward providing opportunities for those emblazoned with the crimson character F.

One needs to understand that life is different after Club Fed. Uncle Sam has taken care of you while on sabbatical and now it is the culprit's time to avoid reoccurring behavior.

Stay positive. Stay active. Stay focused. AND, by all means, avoid becoming a Repeat Offender!

Scarlet Success Stories (SSS)

Don't let the Scarlet F hold you back from realizing your dreams. Take it from this crimson crew who, after sabbatical, went on to become more successful......

Robert Downey Jr (Corcoran II)
Actor
(other crimson actors include Danny Trejo, Christian Slater, Tim Allen...to name a few)

Dinesh D'Souza (HWH)
Author and Political Commentator

Frizzle Gerald Gray (aka Kweisi Mfume)
Congressman, President NAACP

Jeff Henderson (FCI Terminal Island)
Chef

Curtis James Jackson III (aka 50 Cent) (Several)
Musician/Rapper

Steve Madden (FPC Eglin and Coleman FCC)
Creative and Design Chief Steve Madden Inc.

Nelson Mandela (Robben Island)
Former President of South Africa

Martha Stewart (Alderson FPC)
CEO MSLO (Martha Stewart Living Omnimedia)

Michael Vick (USP Leavenworth)
Former NFL Quarterback

Turn your SOS into an SSS!!!!

Never Say Never

Now that you are a Lifetime member of Club F you will **never** be able to do the following:

-Own a gun (no, you can't, but that guy that was locked up in a mental institution for 5 years, he can)

-Participate in Jury Duty

-Vote (depends on what state you live in...hello California!)

-Visit Canada (eh, not so bad..skiing is better in Switzerland anyway)

-Take the bar/become a Lawyer (I know, it seems so easy to pass now that you've been through the entire process of Club Fed...talk about practical experience)

-Run for/Hold office (Chappaquiddick anyone? Had it happened today tipsy Teddy Kennedy would never have been Senator)

The Scarlet F **will** still allow you to do the following:

-Travel to Mexico and the Caribbean (Cerveza por favor!)

-Vote in Maine and Vermont while on sabbatical (they actually set up booth at camp)

-Lounge on the beach in Phuket (or if you prefer, the Cote d'Azur) or track the big 5 in Kruger

**Disclaimer...change is on the horizon....be aware of legislation under review. For instance, while the states of Kentucky, Virginia and Florida have a life time denial on the right to vote currently several Criminal Justice Reform efforts are underway to change the laws. Fortunately there are lots of politicos that are WCCs and they are pushing for reform in a major way.

Wonderful
Crimson
Charities

(Another WCC!)

Wonderful Crimson Charities (Another WCC!)

There are an abundance of ways to support members of the WCC taking sabbatical at Club Fed!

Listed below are a few of the volunteer organizations helping support education for those bearing the Scarlet F. Some accept books but others would prefer postage or monetary donations to pay for shipping costs.

Books to Prisoners (est. 1973) is a Seattle area non-profit that mails free books to prisoners in the U.S. Check out their website (www.bookstoprisoners.net) and Twitter feed (@B2PSeattle).

Another great provider of educational materials to women in prisons nationwide is **Chicago Books to Women in Prison**. Please view their website (www.Chicagobwp.org) to see what books are needed or email them (chicagobwp@gmail.com) and follow them on Twitter (@ChicagoBWP).

DC Books to Prisons is part of the Washington Peace Center and since 1999 has provided free books to prisoners as well as prison libraries. Please check their website (dcbookstoprisoners.org) to donate and follow them on Twitter (@B2Pdc).

Books Through Bars was established in 1990 and is an all volunteer non-profit organization that sends free books to prisoners. Located in Philadelphia they can be reached at info@booksthroughbars.org or view their Twitter posts (@btbphilly) or check out their website for donation suggestions (booksthroughbars.org).

Inside Books Project is an Austin, Texas based non-profit founded in 1998 that sends free books and educational materials to people in Texas prisons. Review their website (InsideBooksProject.org) or follow them on Twitter (@InsideBooksATX) or email them to find out what special requests they may have ((insidebooksproject@gmail.com).

Prison Book Program @prisonbookprog, prisonbookprogram.org

Free Minds Book Club @FreeMindsDC, freemindsbookclub.org

CT Prison Books @CTPrisonBooks. Website currently under development but donations can be sent to CT Prison Books, PO Box 946, Rocky Hill, CT 06067-0946

Liberation Library @liberationlib. Based in Chicago, this group provides books to youth in Illinois prisons. Visit their website (liberationlib.com) or visit them at Liberation Library @ In These Times, 2040 N. Milwaukee Ave., Chicago, IL 60647.

Louisville Books to Prisoners can be contacted at louisvillebtp@gmail.com or 502-625-LB2P and you can also view their website at louisvillebooksto-prisoners.org. Donations can be sent to McQuixote Books & Coffee, 1512 Portland Avenue #1, Louisville, KY 40203 Attn: Louisville Books to Prisoners.

"Education is the most powerful weapon which you can use to change the world" - Nelson Mandela

The WCC Cookbook

Ingrid Lederhaas-Okun

The WCC Cookbook.....coming soon!

Do you need to ask "Alexa" how long it takes to boil eggs?

Well, there is no Amazon Echo at Club Fed so The WCC Handbook has compiled a "How To" book for those that are cooking challenged.

While you may encounter a fellow camp mate that has taken some courses at the CIA (no, not that one...The Culinary Institute of America), should you not be that fortunate it's best to read up on how to prepare the basics, as the meals Uncle Sam provides can be quite repetitive.

One might be surprised to find out that Fed Mart has a vast assortment of items available for purchase that can, with the proper instructions, make for meals that even Bobby Flay would find appetizing! No, not on the level of Daniel Bouley, but certainly Alton Brown would be impressed!

In need of some comfort food after a particularly draining phone call? Whip up some creamy mac and cheese!

Care to celebrate your team's Super Bowl win? How about some 'no bake' chocolate chip or oatmeal cookies?

Feeling a little under the weather? Some spicy chicken soup may do the trick.

Hosting a birthday party? Try the delicious chocolate Oreo cake with caramel swirls.

Whatever your Crimson craving you will find recipes from Beginner to Advanced with step by step instructions.

An excerpt to whet your appetite....follow @thewcchandbook for future publication date!

M Stew Eat your Heart Out

Necessity is the mother of invention...no truer words were ever spoken... especially when ensconced at Club Fed.

Should you wish to try your hand at "cooking" try the following Camp friendly recipes.

Banana Layer Cake

*Ingredients**
One package Pound Cake Loaf
One package Vanilla (or Chocolate) Pudding (3 cups per package)
Two Sliced Bananas
One Dole Tropical Fruit Cup Diced
Two packages Cream Cheese
Cinnamon Crunch Cereal (or equivalent)
Chocolate Syrup (optional)
Plastic Tupperware Rectangular Dish
Two Plastic Round Bowls
Plastic knife, spoon and fork

Instructions
Slice pound cake and place several slices on bottom of a rectangular plastic dish to create bottom layer of cake
In a separate plastic bowl combine pudding with drained diced fruit (safe the juice!)
In a separate plastic bowl use juice from fruit cup and mix with cream cheese until smooth and creamy
Fold the cream cheese mixture into the pudding mixture
Pour the blended mixture to just cover the top of the pound cake
Place banana slices on top of pudding/cream cheese mixture

Layer another slice of pound cake and repeat until all pound cake is used or container can not hold any more layers
Chill for several hours (encase in ice from ice machine)

Before serving, sprinkle crushed Cinnamon Crunch cereal (or drizzle chocolate syrup) on top

Cake Pops

Ingredients**
One package Pound Cake Loaf
One XL Chocolate Bar (if no XL available use 3-4 smaller bars)
Several packages Cream Cheese
Fluff Marshmallow (you will have to judge amount based upon texture of dough)
Creamer
Butter
2 packages Candy (Reese's Pieces, M & M's or equivalent)
Three Plastic Tupperware Bowls
6-8 Sticks (wooden or plastic)

Instructions
In a bowl crush Pound Cake
Add Cream Cheese and Fluff to crushed Pound Cake until it becomes doughy
Roll the dough into small balls and pierce with stick (like a lollipop)
Place lollipops in clean bowl and chill dough balls on stick
While lollipops are chilling, in a separate bowl melt chocolate in microwave and mix in butter and creamer until it resembles a chocolate ganache
In a separate bowl crush Candy into little bits
Take chilled lollipops and dip them in warm ganache then roll them in candy
You can either serve warm (if you can't resist them any longer) or let them chill again then serve

ENJOY!

**Please note that ingredients vary depending upon locale (substitute based upon Fed Mart selections)

TheWCCHandbook.com

Please visit TheWCCHandbook.com website for blog updates and future ECommerce items. Proceeds go toward educating the incarcerated.

@thewcchandbook

Follow The WCC Handbook on Twitter for articles pertaining to providing second chances to bearers of The Scarlet F, including employment and education opportunities.

TheWCCHandbook@gmail.com

All other inquiries should be addressed via email to thewcchandbook@gmail.com

Author Bio:

Ingrid Lederhaas-Okun is a former executive of a luxury jewelry company and a WCC. She has created The WCC Handbook after a brief sabbatical at Alderson FPC to provide a whimsical look at the Club Fed experience. An avid believer in second chances, she supports organizations providing educational support to bearers of The Scarlet F.